Ju

ELE

SPELLS

GUIDEBOOK

GW01455023

ELEMENTAL SPELLS

ELEMENTAL
SPELLS

Drawing on the Magical Energy of
Fire, Earth, Air, and Water

Julieta Suárez Valente

Red
Wheel

This edition first published in 2025 by Red Wheel, an imprint of
Red Wheel/Weiser, LLC
With offices at:
65 Parker Street, Suite 7
Newburyport, MA 01950
www.redwheelweiser.com

Copyright © 2019 by FERA/Julieta Suárez Valente
Translation copyright © 2025 by Red Wheel/Weiser

All rights reserved. No part of this publication may be reproduced or
transmitted in any form or by any means, electronic or mechanical,
including photocopying, recording, or by any information storage and
retrieval system, nor used in any manner for purposes of training artifi-
cial intelligence (AI) technologies to generate text or imagery, including
technologies that are capable of generating works in the same style
or genre, without permission in writing from Red Wheel/Weiser, LLC.
Reviewers may quote brief passages. Previously published in 2023 as
Oráculo de hechizos by FERA, ISBN: 978-987-48890-3-4.

ISBN: 978-1-59003-583-2

Illustrations by Miranda Guerrero
Design by Belén Rigou
Typeset in Soin Sans Neue

Printed in China
WMB
10 9 8 7 6 5 4 3 2 1

CONTENTS

How to Use This Oracle 6

Ingredients for Spellwork. 8

The Four Elements 10

Fire 13

Earth 23

Air 33

Water 43

✦ ✦ How to Use This Oracle ✦ ✦

The spells in this oracle offer rituals, recipes, and ways of focusing your intention in order to attract energy for your personal growth: identifying your wishes, as Fire suggests; manifesting as embodied by Earth; having clear ideas as proposed by Air; accepting personal vulnerability as led by Water.

There are two main ways to use this oracle. The first and most traditional is to place the deck on a flat surface, face down; then shuffle, cut, spread out the cards, and draw one or more to receive a message. The second way is to choose a recipe or spell according to the energy you want to invoke. To do so, you will need your cards face up and this guidebook to identify the essence of the four elements. On pages 21, 31, 41, and 51, you will find summaries of the forty-four spells.

+ Spreads:

Spreads are another way to work with the deck, using one, three, or five cards.

1. Single card: This reading focuses on one card. The oracle reflects the situation you are going through and offers you advice in the form of a powerful message.

2. Past, present, and future: This reading is useful in identifying the energetic processes you are going through: where you come from, where you are now, and where you are headed.

3. Cross: This reading offers you a complete overview of how energies are linked. In this case, it is ideal to observe which element is prevalent or if there is a balance or combination of elements. The following questions will be addressed.

1. **Where do I come from?**
2. **Where am I going?**
3. **What is my state of mind?**
4. **What are my fears?**
5. **What does my present situation look like?**

Ingredients for Spellwork

Herbs and Aromatics

- **Rosemary** (herbs or essential oil)
- **Lavender** (flowers, essential oil, spray, or cream)
- **Essential oil of lavender, eucalyptus, sandalwood, or jasmine**
- **Dried buds of Chinese rose and rose hips**
- **Rose petals** (and their essential oil)
- **Lemon**
- **Bay leaves**
- **Ginger**

Stones and Crystals

- **Sodalite**
- **Quartz**
- **Pink quartz**
- **Pyrite**
- **Tiger eye**
- **Citrine**

Colored Candles

- **Orange:** for intellect, justice, and celebrations
- **Purple:** for psychic skills, spirituality, and intuition
- **Blue:** for peace, wisdom, and creativity
- **Red:** for passion, love, and courage
- **Gold:** for wealth, solar energy, and generosity
- **Pink:** for self-love, romance, and friendship

The Four Elements

The four elements—Fire, Earth, Air, and Water—have been used since ancient times to identify different types of energy. Ancient philosophers studied the elements, and, over time, practitioners of magic used them for their different energetic properties. In fact, the four elements are found in astrology, tarot, and witchcraft.

Apart from helping us understand ourselves, we can use the four elements to attract energy. For example, if your Sun and Moon fall under a Water sign, you may be an emotional person who needs to attract the

energy of Earth to your life to carry out projects and fulfill your hopes and dreams. Acknowledging that a Fire ascendant may make someone impulsive, you may see the need to integrate Air energy, like Libra, to infuse a healthy balance.

Throughout this guide, you will find information that will deepen your knowledge about the diverse energies of the elements and guidance for the spells found in the oracle deck.

△

FIRE

FIRE

Fire is a symbol of creativity and passion. It's associated with the energy of action, beginnings, and motivation. You are pushed to achieve your wishes by the vital spark and the fuel that is Fire. It's the divine flame that lights you up, drives your passion, and works to help you achieve your goals. Fire stimulates and enlightens. Invoke it when you feel tired, honor it when your creative juices are flowing, and be thankful when passion takes over.

✦ Fire in Astrology

The Fire signs in astrology are Aries, Leo, and Sagittarius. All three are associated with power and action, although they differ in practice. Aries is characterized by impulsive action and the power to start things up. This kind of energy can be messy, or even wild, when left unchecked. Leo is related to personal expression. Its Fire is aimed at showing off the ego. Its dark side can be self-centered and selfish. Lastly, Sagittarius is a sage Fire sign that seeks growth, travel, and transformation. In excess, Sagittarius can be abrasively overconfident or optimistically deny reality.

The planets associated with Fire are the Sun, Mars, and Jupiter. The Sun makes you light up, energetically speaking. Mars fights the battles for what you want, while Jupiter helps you expand your beliefs.

✦ Wands

In tarot, wands represent the energy of Fire. In the Major Arcana, The Magician uses a wand as an instrument to perform magic. In the Minor Arcana, wands are illustrated as an extension of the body, capable of creating. In modern culture, the use of wands has been popularized in sagas like Harry Potter, where each character has a wand of a given kind of wood and core, matching their character and the magic they will perform.

✦ Candles

Candles are some of the most accessible tools for practicing magic. With the arrival of electricity, they lost their prominence and their practical function. Although they are currently used as decoration or as backup lighting in case of a blackout, candles will always have the ritualizing quality of transforming darkness into light.

Several cards throughout this oracle recommend lighting candles of different colors in order to invoke diverse kinds of energy, and you will find that the ritual of lighting candles is not exclusive to the element of Fire and its qualities.

✴ The Cauldron

Historically utilized by ancient witches, the cauldron was used not only to prepare meals but also to make all kinds of concoctions, both magical and mundane. The heat of the fire underneath melts, cooks, or combines the ingredients in the cauldron and alchemizes their properties. The cauldron is a powerful feminine symbol and represents the heat of the soul.

✦ The Devil Archetype

Did you know that one of the definitions of devil is simply "an exuberant spirit," with no mention of, or association with, morality? In fact, we associate the name Lucifer, which means "he who carries light," with the devil because Lucifer was an angel who rebelled against God and was expelled from heaven. It earned him the description of "fallen angel."

Although historically society claimed there was a connection between witchcraft and the devil, this arose from a desire to control and condemn independent women and their sexuality rather than having any basis in reality. Nowadays, some contemporary tarot decks illustrate the Devil in a way that highlights his power of seduction, ambition, and desire rather than presenting it only as a card about cunning, manipulation, or betrayal.

Fire Element Cards

✦ **Mars:** a planet associated with action

✦ **Sekhmet:** Egyptian lioness goddess

✦ **Lemon:** fruit extracts for an energy boost

✦ **Bay Leaves:** a purification ritual

✦ **Citrine:** crystal-activated water

✦ **Ginger:** a powerful plant from Southeast Asia

✦ **The Sun:** nineteenth Major Arcana

✦ **Sowilo:** Viking rune representing the sun

✦ **New Moon in a Fire Sign:** Aries, Leo, or Sagittarius

✦ **Cauldron:** to burn what we no longer need

✦ **Tiger:** symbol of vital force

Spells for Fire Element

+ **Mars:** to take action
+ **Sekhmet:** to get rid of anger
+ **Lemon:** to enhance your vital force
+ **Bay Leaves:** for purification
+ **Citrine:** to heal your solar plexus
+ **Ginger:** to boost your energy
+ **The Sun:** to get your authenticity back
+ **Sowilo:** to overcome obstacles
+ **New Moon in a Fire Sign:** to give you the courage you need
+ **Cauldron:** to transmute matter
+ **Tiger:** to gather your willpower

EARTH

EARTH

The Earth element is a symbol of manifestation and realization. It's associated with all matter, our bodies, and, of course, our planet. It represents stability and support. Earth's energy shows us that there's power in discipline, determination, and endurance. Rather than rushing and being careless, focusing on slow and steady progress will help you build a solid foundation to accomplish your goals.

✦ Earth in Astrology

The Earth signs are Taurus, Virgo, and Capricorn. These signs are connected to the physical Earth and are expressed in several ways. Taurus is widely known for representing stubbornness but also slowing down and enjoying life's simple pleasures, like sleeping and eating. Virgo is characterized by organizational skills and reasoning but sometimes obsesses over perfection. Finally, Capricorn is known for ambition but also caution and practicality. It's important for Capricorns to avoid putting too much pressure on themselves.

The planets associated with the Earth element are Venus, which offers pleasure and appreciation, and Saturn, which sets up structure, boundaries, and authority.

✦ Ground Yourself According to the Tarot

One of the most classic associations between tarot and the Earth element is The Hermit, the ninth card in the Major Arcana. In this card, we see a wise man who isolates himself to search for the answers that will feed his soul. Such a retreat to solitude will result in good things for the community—a gesture of service—when The Hermit returns to the world with his newly acquired knowledge.

In the Minor Arcana, Earth is associated with the suit of Pentacles. This suit reflects on different ways of relating to resources—often financial. For example, the Ace of Pentacles represents the ability to manifest abundance. The Four of Pentacles invites you to save. The Ten of Pentacles usually means your life is on the right track.

✦ Properties of Nature

Putting your feet in the dirt or sand, hugging a tree, walking through the woods, or hiking a mountain are all ways of connecting with the Earth element. Connection to nature seems far away from us when we live in hectic cities or when we get busy with life. However, nature is closer than we think. Purchase local produce when you can, avoid ultra-processed foods, and support conservationism. As individuals, we usually feel we can't change the world or improve the planet's health. That's not true. It starts with you and spreads to your whole community. Be the one to take the first step!

✦ Herbalism

Herbalism is an age-old practice that uses plants and herbs to heal ailments. Practicing herbalism reconnects you to the green energy of the planet. Two easy-to-access herbs, chamomile and lavender, can provide a simple way to bring the healing power of plants into your daily life. Chamomile is an anti-inflammatory that can be used in compresses to reduce swelling. You can also soak tired feet in a bowl of water with fresh or dried chamomile in it. The scent of lavender has relaxing properties, and it is a good practice to keep both dry and fresh lavender in your bedroom to help you sleep.

✦ Managing Resources

Earth as an element is associated with managing your resources, such as your home, your food, your finances, your body, and your time. Ask yourself about the quality of food you are eating, if you honor your home as a sacred space, if you manage your income responsibly, treat your body with love, or balance your time appropriately. Taking stock of all of these things will help you connect to Mother Nature. Remember, we humans are nothing but a link in an energetic chain of life on Earth.

Earth Element Cards

- **Saturn:** a planet associated with materialization
- **Aphrodite:** Greek goddess of love and sensuality
- **Financial Healing:** recirculation of matter
- **Maneki-neko:** cat figurine
- **Gaia:** primitive Mother Earth goddess
- **Fortuna:** goddess of luck and fertility
- **Smiling Buddha:** icon of Eastern wisdom
- **Turtle:** Mother Earth's wisdom and support
- **Archangel Uriel:** ruler of the ruby-gold flame
- **Berkana:** Viking rune of spring
- **Pyrite:** a mineral that facilitates energetic flow

Spells for Earth Element

✦ **Saturn:** to make wishes reality

✦ **Aphrodite:** to invoke your connection to your body

✦ **Financial Healing:** to balance your relationship with money

✦ **Maneki-neko:** to attract good fortune

✦ **Gaia:** to help keep a solid footing

✦ **Fortuna:** to connect to abundance

✦ **Smiling Buddha:** to change the vibration in the room

✦ **Turtle:** to invoke tenacity

✦ **Archangel Uriel:** to get a good outcome

✦ **Berkana:** to flourish

✦ **Pyrite:** to attract money and self-esteem

AIR

✦ AIR ✦

As an element, Air is associated with thought, ideas, and communication. It is the energetic neural network that connects all things, allowing us to learn, listen, speak, write, and think. Air is a linking element. It reminds you that the power of your mind and words have vibration and magnetism. Air is agile, fast, and lively—it's constantly moving. Breathing air gives us life and keeps us connected to others.

✦ Air in Astrology

The Air signs are Gemini, Libra, and Aquarius. All three signs are considered light and ephemeral, and they have difficulty achieving goals. Each of them has a different relationship with the abstract element of Air. Gemini seeks ideas, change, and multiplicity. A negative aspect of Gemini can be summarized by the phrase "holding much but possessing little." In Libra, Air circulates to gently strengthen relationships. In its negative aspect, Libra can become condescending. Finally, in Aquarius, Air focuses on connecting to a community; this sign understands the importance of social interaction. However, sometimes they can be too enthusiastic.

The planets related to Air are Mercury, which is in charge of communication, and Uranus, which is the champion of upheaval and shifts in consciousness.

◆ Swords

In the Major Arcana, the Justice card is associated with Air. Justice is also related to Libra in its search for harmony, represented in the card by the presence of a balanced scale. However, the woman in Justice also has a big sword representing subjectivity. This tool allows her to cut to the chase, pass judgment, and decide who comes in and out of her life. Justice can be either fair or authoritarian. If she cannot regulate the use of her sword, she can hurt others.

In the Minor Arcana, the suit of Swords will present ideas which may be elaborated on or argued for.

✦ Flight and a Meditation

In the past, it was thought that witches were capable of flying from one place to another on brooms. However, what flight really represents is the ability to rise above everyday issues and seek freedom; the air space is not ruled by laws imposed by man. Air is for those who dare to escape regular routines that hold them back or suppress them.

To "fly" you must enter a meditative state and connect to only yourself in the present moment. Breathe in varying rhythms, which will help you relax and feel a positive change in your state of awareness.

+ Power Animals with Wings

Power animals are beings that help guide us to other realms. We are usually introduced to them via meditation or visualization. After we have identified a power animal, we can name it, then invoke it whenever we need magical assistance.

Among the numerous winged power animals, the most popular ones are the owl (capable of offering you information), the eagle (offering vision and mental clarity), the hummingbird (representing intelligence and versatility), and the raven (master of mysticism and hidden knowledge).

✦ Words

Did you know the word *abracadabra* literally means "I create as I speak"? Both writing and speaking have the power to heal, change an outcome, and invoke desires. Writing down an intention on a piece of paper to burn it or freeze it, carving words into candles to attract things, saying a prayer; these are just some of the many ways of using language in magic.

Therapeutic writing—keeping diaries and having a record of your life—is another way of ritualizing your words.

Air Element Cards

+ **Quartz:** an energy-magnifying mineral
+ **Mercury:** the planet of communication
+ **Ace of Swords:** tarot's Minor Arcana
+ **Athena:** Greek goddess of wisdom
+ **Owl:** intellectual power and practical talent
+ **New Moon in an Air Sign:** Gemini, Libra, or Aquarius
+ **Rosemary:** an herb for concentration
+ **Aeolus:** Greek god of wind
+ **Archangel Jophiel:** golden ray of enlightenment
+ **Ansuz:** Viking rune for communication
+ **Crystal Healing:** to empower your voice

Spells for Air Element

- ✦ **Quartz:** to clear doubt
- ✦ **Mercury:** for good communication and unblocking creativity
- ✦ **Ace of Swords:** to cut off limiting thoughts
- ✦ **Athena:** for self-confidence
- ✦ **Owl:** to bring new information and remove anxieties
- ✦ **New Moon in an Air Sign:** to generate ideas for new projects
- ✦ **Rosemary:** for concentration
- ✦ **Aeolus:** to set stuck energy into motion
- ✦ **Archangel Jophiel:** to connect to your talent
- ✦ **Ansuz:** to find agreement
- ✦ **Crystal Healing:** to heal and clarify your voice

WATER

WATER

As an element, Water is a symbol of emotional energy, intuition, and depth. It is associated with feelings and spirituality. Water reminds us that we are in a state of constant movement, like waves, and that feeling deeply is a symbol of strength and courage. Sensitivity is a great gift that grants you empathy and love and enables you to navigate mysteries that are not easy to understand.

✦ Water in Astrology

The Water signs in astrology are Cancer, Scorpio, and Pisces. Cancer tends to develop emotions in a more intimate environment. There is often a strong desire to start a family and to have a sense of belonging. Keep in mind, though, that maternal or paternal instincts can be too intense if they are not reined in. Scorpio makes everything very personal. Intuition gets sharper, and there is a lot of soul searching. This can be a bit too intense for some people. Finally, Pisces's strength is expanding empathy until it reaches every being in the world. But be warned: that sensitivity can become overwhelming.

The planets associated with Water are the Moon, shelter of all vulnerability; Pluto, lord of the depths of the soul; and Neptune, in charge of softening rigid boundaries and allowing pure flow of consciousness.

✦ From Contained to Flowing Waters

The effect of Water is represented by three Major Arcana cards in the tarot. In Temperance, the fourteenth card, there's a winged woman, or an angel, pouring water from one pot to another. There, the water is contained and that represents emotional balance. In The Star, the seventeenth card, water in the pots is poured into a river. The woman is offering her gift to the universe by sharing her knowledge. The Moon, the eighteenth card, is the most emotional card. In it, we see a winding river through which our dreams dance, intermingled with our fears. Who dares enter the darkness of the night, to get lost and have only the river as your guide?

✦ Cups and Chalices

As we know, water has no shape. It adopts the shape of the vessel in which it is contained. That's why chalices have a prominent role in the history of sorcery. Chalices are used in ceremonies to carry sacred liquids (like holy water) and potions.

In the tarot, the suit of Cups in the Minor Arcana represents the sensitive nature of water. Cups cards show you diverse ways of interacting with the role of Water signs. Give it your all (Ace of Cups), share your inner world (Three of Cups), travel to a nostalgic past (Six of Cups), and even escape from reality (Seven of Cups).

✦ Baths

A very simple ancient way of carrying out a magical ritual is a purification bath. Water washes the body, removing everything you no longer need to carry or support. Remember: within the four elements, water has the power of transformation and is the only one that's capable of turning from liquid to gas or solid. Although baths typically refer to immersing yourself in water, taking a shower with the right ingredients can serve the same purpose. The ingredients can be bath salts, herbs, flowers, oils, or crystals, depending on what you want to cleanse.

✴ Potions

In the Middle Ages, botanical preparations were closely related to natural medicine. They were tinctures and tonics with healing power. As botanical knowledge progressed, the psychoactive use of these herbs was extended and people used them to alter their state of consciousness.

There are healing potions that can easily be prepared, like ginger tea with garlic and honey for a sore throat, chamomile and dandelion infusions for indigestion, and arnica ointment for muscle pain.

Water Element Cards

- **Lavender:** a flower for harmony
- **Kwan Yin:** Chinese goddess
- **Third Eye:** Ajna chakra
- **Archangel Chamuel:** pink ray of divine love
- **Whale:** symbol of emotional depth
- **New Moon in a Water Sign:** Cancer, Scorpio, or Pisces
- **Love Talisman:** protective Viking symbol
- **The Hanged Man:** twelfth Major Arcana
- **Crystal Therapy:** for emotional healing
- **Dream Journal:** discover important messages
- **Harmony:** rose petal bath

Spells for Water Element

* **Lavender:** to encourage awareness of self-care
* **Kwan Yin:** to invoke compassion
* **Third Eye:** to connect to your inner wisdom
* **Archangel Chamuel:** to invoke love
* **Whale:** to dive into your subconscious world
* **New Moon in a Water Sign:** to become more intuitive
* **Love Talisman:** to heal heartbreak
* **The Hanged Man:** for silencing your mind
* **Crystal Therapy:** to heal rejection or separation
* **Dream Journal:** to connect to your subconscious
* **Harmony:** for emotional cleansing

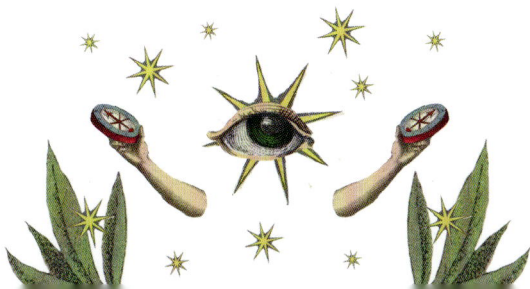

About the Creators

Author

Julieta Suárez Valente is an Argentine writer, astrologer, and tarot reader. She has deep knowledge of a variety of symbolic languages: mythology, runes, shamanism, chakras, arcana, and healing, among other things. She is the author of *Vibrate Higher*. *Elemental Spells* gathers all of Julieta's mysticism in these forty-four cards to help you with your magical practice. @astrologia_y_consciencia

✦ Illustrator

Miranda Guerrero is a Mexican artist who creates digital collages inspired by witches, esoterism, and feminism. She makes use of a vintage aesthetic to approach magical thinking from an anthropological point of view, showing us that destiny can be changed only by us.
@mirandacollage

To Our Readers

Based on the symbolism of the wheel, Red Wheel offers books and divination decks from a variety of traditions. We aim to provide the ideas, information, and innovative approaches to help you develop your own spiritual path.

Please visit our website *www.redwheelweiser.com* to learn more about our full range of titles.

Red Wheel/Weiser, LLC
65 Parker Street, Suite 7
Newburyport, MA 01950
www.redwheelweiser.com